To:

~~~~~~~~~~~~~~~~~~~~~~

From:

~~~~~~~~~~~~~~~~~~~~~~

Date:

~~~~~~~~~~~~~~~~~~~~~~

The grass withers and the flowers fall,
but the word of the Lord endures forever.

1 Peter 1:24-25

Published by Christian Art Publishers
PO Box 1599, Vereeniging, 1930, RSA

© 2016
First edition 2016

Designed by Christian Art Publishers

Images used under license from Shutterstock.com

Printed in China

ISBN 978-1-4321-1563-0
ISBN 978-1-64272-618-3

20 21 22 23 24 25 26 27 28 29 – 34 33 32 31 30 29 28 27 26 25

The Word in Color

COLORING BOOK

CHRISTIAN ART
PUBLISHERS

I CAN do all things THROUGH Christ WHO GIVES ME strength.

PHILIPPIANS 4:13

GOD'S
Grace
is all
you need.

2 CORINTHIANS 12:9

BE STRONG AND COURAGEOUS FOR THE LORD YOUR GOD WILL BE WITH YOU WHEREVER YOU GO.

JOSHUA 1:9

THE LORD IS MY Strength AND MY Song

Exodus 15:2

THIS IS THE
DAY THAT
THE LORD
HAS MADE;
LET US
REJOICE.
PSALM 118:24

THE moon THE & stars YOU set in place.

PSALM 8:3

TASTE & SEE THAT THE LORD IS GOOD PSALM 34:8

SHE IS clothed WITH Strength AND dignity AND SHE laughs WITHOUT FEAR OF THE future

PROVERBS 31:25

GREAT IS THE LORD & MOST WORTHY OF PRAISE

Psalm 96:4

I HAVE WRITTEN YOUR NAME ON THE PALMS OF MY HANDS

ISAIAH 49:16

BE KIND

KIND WORDS ARE LIKE HONEY - SWEET TO THE SOUL.

PROVERBS 16:24

SET YOUR MINDS ON things ABOVE.

COLOSSIANS 3:2

TRUST IN THE LORD WITH ALL YOUR HEART

PROVERBS 3:5

AS FOR ME AND MY
HOUSE
WE WILL SERVE THE LORD.
Joshua 24:15

UNDER HIS WINGS YOU WILL FIND REFUGE

PSALM 91:4

JEREMIAH 17:7

Blessed
is the one who
TRUSTS
in the
LORD

He refreshes my soul

PSALM 23:3

Live a life filled with love.

EPHESIANS 5:2

Clothe yourselves with compassion kindness humility patience gentleness

COLOSSIANS 3:12

THE LORD IS MY LIGHT & MY SALVATION

PSALM 27:1

EVERY GOOD

& PERFECT

GIFT

IS FROM

ABOVE

JAMES 1:17

CALL TO ME

and I will answer you and tell you great and unsearchable things you do not know.

Jeremiah 33:3

HIS name WILL BE THE hope OF ALL THE WORLD.

MATTHEW 12:21

HE counts the Stars calls them all by Name.

PSALM 147:4

HE WILL cover you with HIS FEATHERS, and under His wings YOU WILL FIND REFUGE.

PSALM 91:4

THE
FAITHFUL
LOVE
OF THE
LORD
NEVER
ENDS
LAMENTATIONS 3:22

FOR IT IS BY

GRACE

YOU HAVE BEEN SAVED

EPHESIANS 2:8

MY CUP OVERFLOWS WITH

Blessings

PSALM 23:5

BOOKMARKS & TAGS
COLOR, CUT, PUNCH AND
TIE A RIBBON

"FOR I *know* the PLANS I HAVE FOR *you.*"

JEREMIAH 29:11

I CAN *do* ALL things THROUGH *Christ* WHO STRENGTHENS *me.*

PHILIPPIANS 4:13

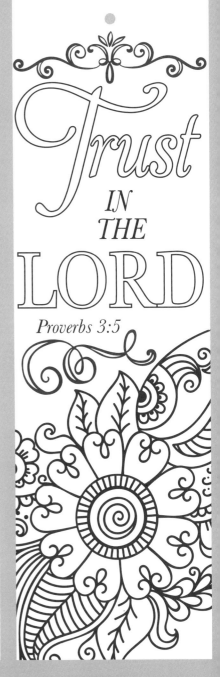

Trust IN THE LORD

Proverbs 3:5

The Lord will guide you always.

Isaiah 58:11

Rejoice in the Lord.

Philippians 4:4

Numbers 6:24

May the Lord BLESS you.

Love
NEVER FAILS.
1 CORINTHIANS 13:8

May you be filled
with joy.

Colossians 1:11

BE GLAD IN THE LORD.
PSALM 32:11